LET'S ROCK!

Science Adventures with Rudie the Origami Dinosaur

by Eric Braun

illustrated by Jamey Christoph

PICTURE WINDOW BOOKS
a capstone imprint

At the party, the kids were making crafts. The Birthday Girl made the final folds on Rudie, her origami dinosaur. Then it was time to bash the piñata!

Rudie and her friend the stick man fell off the table and onto the ground. Rudie looked around.

"The neighborhood sure has changed."

"what do you mean?"

"I'm a dinosaur, silly. I'm from prehistoric times. Back then there were no houses or people here."

"But not everything has changed. These rocks look pretty much the same as always."

"ROCKS? No one notices rocks."

Crust

Mantle

Core

"I do!" cried Rudie. "The crust of Earth is made of solid rock. I was born in a nest of rocks. Did you know rocks are made of **minerals?**"

"**sure, minerals, yeah,**" said the stick man, looking at the piñata. "I hope a piece of **candy** lands over here when they break that thing!"

"There are **three main kinds** of rocks. This one is an **igneous rock**."

"Rocks are rocks. I don't think they're very interesting. If we could get our hands on some **candy**, now **that** would be interesting."

"That **would** be interesting, because **you don't have any hands**."

"Wait, did you say ignorant rock?"

"No, it's an igneous rock. Igneous rocks are formed when lava cools and hardens. As it cools crystals form. You can spot an igneous rock because of its crystals."

"The crystals are kinda cool. Sparkly!"

"I told you rocks were cool!"

Types of
Igneous Rocks

basalt

granite

diorite

pumice

obsidian

"What other kinds of rocks are there?"
asked the stick man.

"Well, there are **sedimentary rocks**, like that one."

Rudie pointed to the big
rock by the raspberry bushes.

"Said a
what?"

"Sedimentary."

Layers of chemicals or tiny rocks and sand are called **sediment**," Rudie continued. "As the layers build up over time, they stick together. Pressure from water or earth hardens the layers into **rocks**."

"So **sediment** makes **sedimentary rocks**."

"**Right**. And sometimes other things, like **fossils**, get stuck in the sediment too. The fossils teach us about living things from long ago."

Types of Sedimentary Rocks

breccia

sandstone

shale

limestone

"NOW, metamorphic rocks are made by heat and pressure deep inside Earth. The heat and pressure cause many rocks to melt together. when the melted mass cools, it is a metamorphic rock."

"so a bunch of rocks become one?"

"yes, look at this metamorphic rock."

"It looks like marble," said the stick man.

"It sure does!" said Rudie. "Marble is one kind of metamorphic rock. It used to be limestone."

"Wait, are metamorphic rocks the same as sedimentary rocks? You said sedimentary rocks are made of stuff like small rocks that harden under pressure, and metamorphic rocks are made by heat and pressure. What's the difference?"

"You're right. But metamorphic rocks form when other rocks are melted together. Sedimentary rocks stay solid. They may get hot when pressed together, but not hot enough to melt."

diamond

graphite

Types of
**Metamorphic
Rocks**

marble

schist

quartzite

gneiss

"Look at all the candy!" shouted the stick man. "It's like a **candy volcano exploded!**"

"Well, if it were a **real volcano**, we'd see **hot lava** forming igneous rocks right now. It's one way rocks change. **Wind, water, heat, chemicals,** and **pressure** can change rocks too. They just do it more slowly."

"DO you miss the old days?" asked the stick man.

"A little," Rudie said. "The rocks here remind me of my old nest in the rocks. But it will be nice to live inside a house."

"Maybe, but I think I'll bring this sparkly igneous rock with me. It'll be the first rock in my new collection."

"Good idea! Your collection will be my new nest."

GLOSSARY

core—the inner part of Earth that is made of metal, rocks, and melted rock

crust—the hard outer layer of Earth

crystal—a body that is formed when certain substances change into a solid

fossil—the remains or traces of an animal or a plant, preserved as rock

igneous—rock that was once melted rock within Earth, then cooled and hardened

lava—the hot liquid rock that pours out of a volcano when it erupts; also called magma

mantle—the layer of hot rock between Earth's crust and the core

metamorphic—rock that is changed by heat and pressure

mineral—a material found in nature that is not an animal or a plant

prehistoric—living or occurring in a time before history was written down

sedimentary—rock formed by layers of rocks, sand, or clay that have been pressed together

READ MORE

Brown, Cynthia Light, and Nick Brown. *Explore Rocks and Minerals!* White River Junction, Vt.: Nomad Press, 2010.

O'Neal, Claire. *A Project Guide to Rocks and Minerals.* Earth Science Projects for Kids. Hockessin, Del.: Mitchell Lane Pub., 2011.

Tomecek, Steve. *Rocks and Minerals.* Jump into Science. Washington, D.C.: National Geographic Society, 2010.

MAKE AN ORIGAMI T. REX

Rudie is a rockin' T. rex! Want to make your own chomping dinosaur? Check out these instructions.

what you Need

8 1/2 x 11 paper

WHAT YOU DO

Folds

valley folds are shown with a dashed line. One side of the paper is folded against the other like a book. A sharp fold is made by running your finger along the fold line.

Arrows

single-pointed arrow: Fold the paper in the direction of the arrow.

double-pointed arrow: Fold the paper and the unfold it.

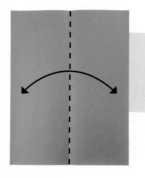

1. Valley fold the left edge to the right edge and unfold.

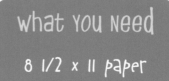

2. Valley fold the top edge to the bottom edge.

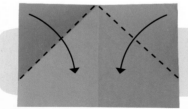

3. Valley fold the top corners to the center fold.

4. Valley fold both bottom edges. Note how the folds meet the edges of the triangles.

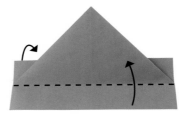

5. Pull the bottom edges apart to allow the model to flatten. The model will become a square.

6. Valley fold both bottom points to the top point.

7. Pull the bottom edges apart to allow the model to flatten. The model will become a square once again.

8. Pinch the top points of the model. Gently pull the points apart to flatten the model into a sailboat.

9. Tuck the center triangle under one of the sailboat's inside flaps.

10. Gently pinch the slanting sides of the sailboat. Slowly push the sides together until they meet.

INDEX

Look for all the books in the series:

Diggin' Dirt: Science Adventures with Kitanai the Origami Dog

Let's Rock!: Science Adventures with Rudie the Origami Dinosaur

Magnet Power!: Science Adventures with MAG-3000 the Origami Robot

Plant Parts Smarts: Science Adventures with Charlie the Origami Bee

Thanks to our advisers for their expertise, research, and advice:
Paul McDaniel
Professor of Soil Science
Soil & Land Resources Division
University of Idaho

Terry Flaherty, PhD, Professor of English
Minnesota State University, Mankato

Editor: Shelly Lyons
Designer: Ashlee Suker
Art Director: Nathan Gassman
Production Specialist: Eric Manske
The illustrations in this book were created digitally.

Picture Window Books are published by Capstone,
1710 Roe Crest Drive, North Mankato, Minnesota 56003
www.capstonepub.com

Library of Congress Cataloging-in-Publication Data
Braun, Eric, 1971-
Let's rock! : science adventures with Rudie the origami dinosaur / by Eric Braun ; illustrated by Jamey Christoph.
pages cm. — (Origami science adventures)
Audience: K to grade 3
ISBN 978-1-4048-7971-3 (library binding)
ISBN 978-1-4048-8068-9 (paperback)
ISBN 978-1-4795-0001-7 (eBook PDF)
1. Rocks—Juvenile literature. 2. Origami—Juvenile literature.
I. Christoph, James, illustrator. II. Title.
QE432.2.B73 2013
552—dc23   2012029512

Photo credits:
Digital illustrations include royalty-free images from iStock and Shutterstock.
Capstone Studio: Karon Dubke, 22-23; Shutterstock: Alexey Bragin, 9 (granite), Boris Franz, 9 (pumice), broukoid, 17 (diamond), infografick, 9 (top), Madlen, 17 (marble), Michal Baranski, 13 (limestone, sandstone), Tyler Boyes, 9 (basalt, obsidian), 13 (breccia, shale), 17 (gneiss, graphite, quartzite, schist), voljurij, 9 (diorite)

Printed in the United States of America in Brainerd, Minnesota.
092012   006938BANGS13

INTERNET SITES

FactHound offers a safe, fun way to find Internet sites related to this book. All of the sites on FactHound have been researched by our staff.

Here's all you do:

Visit *www.facthound.com*

Type in this code: 9781404879713